Hungry Hoppers

Grasshoppers in Your Backyard

Written by Nancy Loewen
Illustrated by Brandon Reibeling

Backyard Bugs

Thanks to our advisers for their expertise, research, knowledge, and advice:

Gary A. Dunn, M.S., Director of Education
Young Entomologists' Society
Lansing, Michigan

Susan Kesselring, M.A., Literacy Educator
Rosemount-Apple Valley-Eagan (Minnesota) School District

PICTURE WINDOW BOOKS
Minneapolis, Minnesota

Managing Editor: Bob Temple
Creative Director: Terri Foley
Editors: Nadia Higgins, Brenda Haugen
Editorial Adviser: Andrea Cascardi
Copy Editor: Laurie Kahn
Designer: Nathan Gassman
Page production: Picture Window Books
The illustrations in this book were prepared digitally.

Picture Window Books
5115 Excelsior Boulevard
Suite 232
Minneapolis, MN 55416
1-877-845-8392
www.picturewindowbooks.com

Printed in the United States of America.

Library of Congress Cataloging-in-Publication Data
Loewen, Nancy, 1964—
Hungry hoppers : grasshoppers in your backyard / written by Nancy Loewen ; illustrated by
Brandon Reibeling.
p. cm. — (Backyard bugs)
Summary: Describes the physical characteristics, life cycle, and behavior of grasshoppers.
Includes bibliographical references (p.   ) and index.
ISBN 1-4048-0146-4 (hardcover)
1. Grasshoppers—Juvenile literature. [1. Grasshoppers.]
I. Reibeling, Brandon, ill. II. Title.
QL508.A2L64 2003
595.7'26—dc21
                                                              2003006094

Table of Contents

Big Jumpers

Zip! Zing! What is that jumping in the grass?

Whiz! Whir! Grasshoppers! Look at how far they can jump!

If we're very still, maybe we can see a grasshopper close up.

There's one. Look at its back legs. Do you see how big they are? No wonder grasshoppers are such good jumpers!

A grasshopper can jump up to 20 times the length of its body. That's like a person being able to jump over four telephone poles placed end to end!

7

Sensing Danger

Grasshoppers have big eyes, too. They let the grasshopper see things coming up behind it. Those thin stems near the grasshopper's eyes are called antennae. Grasshoppers use those to touch and smell.

A grasshopper always watches out for hungry creatures such as birds, frogs, and lizards. Its senses let it know when an enemy is near so it can quickly hop away.

This grasshopper is called a short-horned grasshopper because of the size of its antennae.

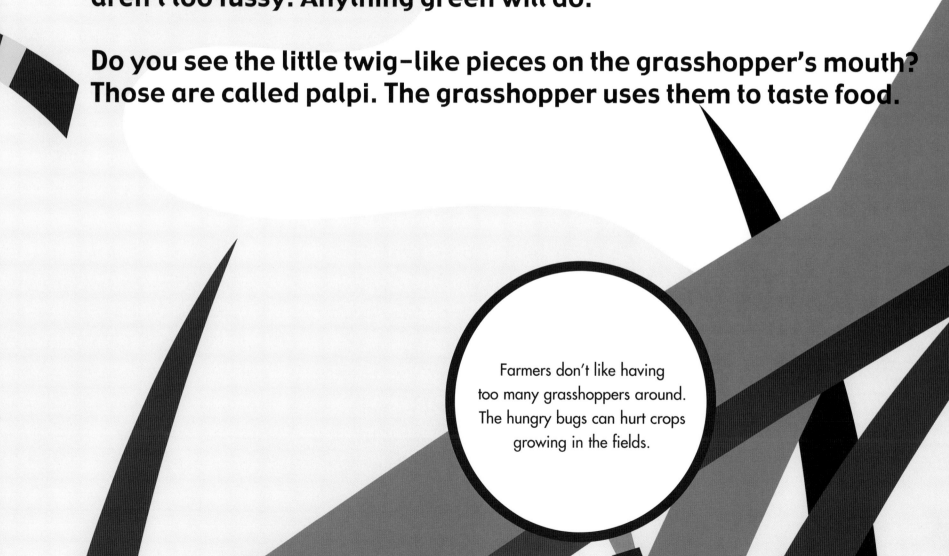

What Do Grasshoppers Eat?

Grasshoppers eat plants of all kinds. Most grasshoppers aren't too fussy. Anything green will do.

Do you see the little twig-like pieces on the grasshopper's mouth? Those are called palpi. The grasshopper uses them to taste food.

Farmers don't like having too many grasshoppers around. The hungry bugs can hurt crops growing in the fields.

Tricky Wings

There's a grasshopper flying away. Can you see its bright wings? Those colorful wings are usually hidden by another pair of dull, outer wings.

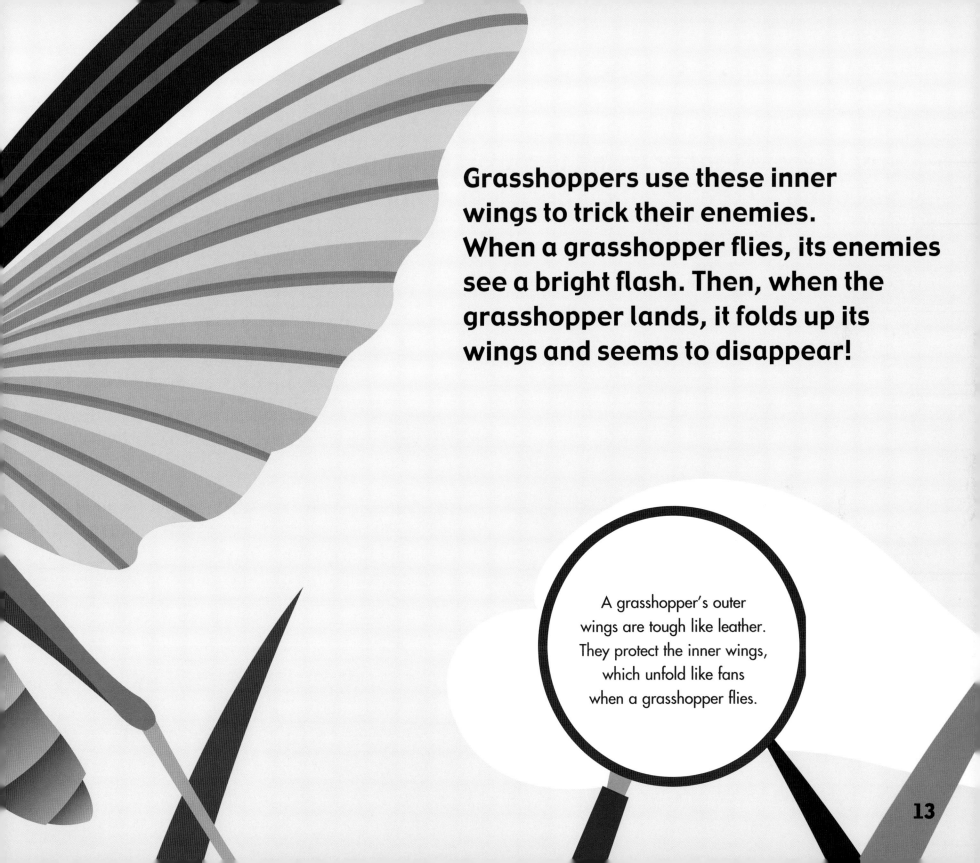

Grasshoppers use these inner wings to trick their enemies. When a grasshopper flies, its enemies see a bright flash. Then, when the grasshopper lands, it folds up its wings and seems to disappear!

A grasshopper's outer wings are tough like leather. They protect the inner wings, which unfold like fans when a grasshopper flies.

13

Life Cycle of a Grasshopper

Shhh. Do you hear that buzzing sound? That's probably a male grasshopper trying to attract a mate. Males make this sound by rubbing their back legs against their wings.

About two weeks after mating, a female grasshopper lays 25 to 150 eggs in the soil. Her body makes a sticky glue that mixes with the soil. When the soil dries, it creates a case that protects the eggs.

A grasshopper's greatest enemy is fly larvae. Fly larvae are little worms that will turn into flies. They often feed on grasshopper eggs.

The grasshoppers die in late autumn, but the eggs live through winter. They hatch in the spring when the ground warms up.

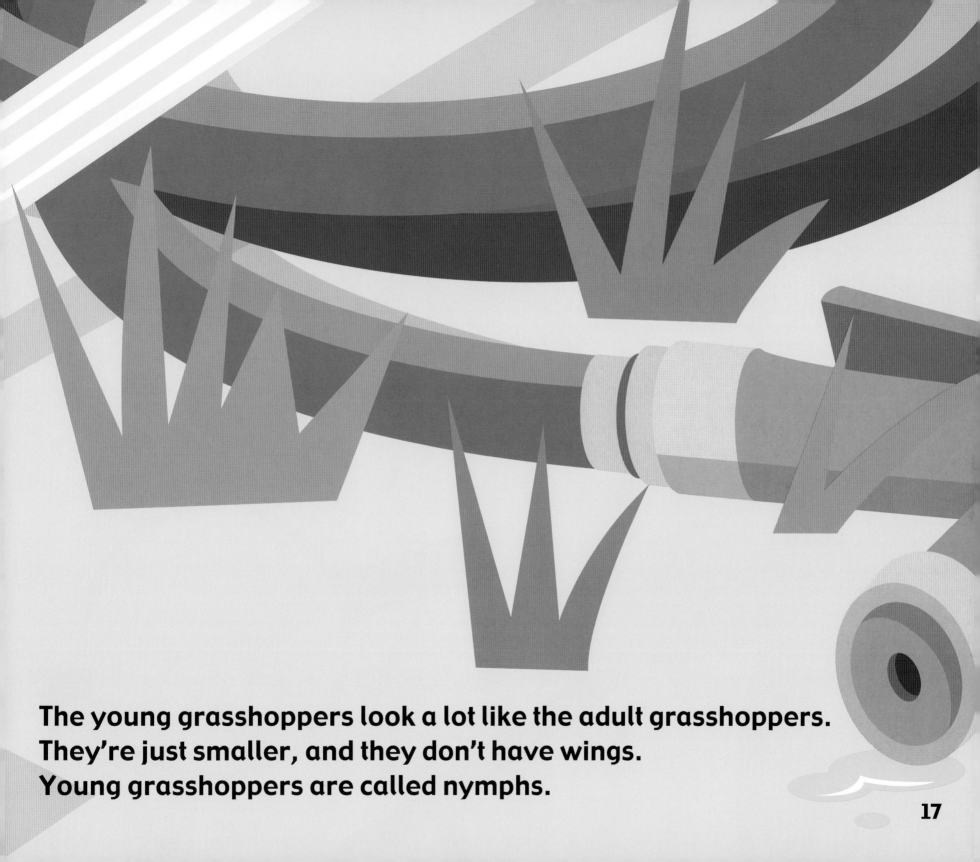

The young grasshoppers look a lot like the adult grasshoppers.
They're just smaller, and they don't have wings.
Young grasshoppers are called nymphs.

The grasshopper nymph eats and eats all summer.
As it grows, its shell gets too small and cracks off.
This is called molting. A new, bigger covering is
underneath the old covering. A nymph molts five
or six times before becoming an adult.

When nymphs first hatch,
they are almost white.
After a few hours, their color
and markings appear.

19

Grasshopper Games

You might not notice grasshoppers much in the spring and early summer. That is when they are small and good at hiding. In late summer and into autumn, the grasshoppers are fully grown. It might seem as if they are everywhere.

Zip! Zing! Go ahead. See if you can catch one!

Look Closely at a Grasshopper

Look at a short-horned grasshopper through a magnifying glass. How many of these different parts can you see?

Antennae are for touching and smelling.
Big **eyes** can see to the front, side, and back.
The **palpus** is for tasting food. Grasshoppers have two palpi.
Green or brown **outer wings** protect the body.
Colorful **inner wings** are for flying.
Like all insects, a grasshopper has six **legs**.

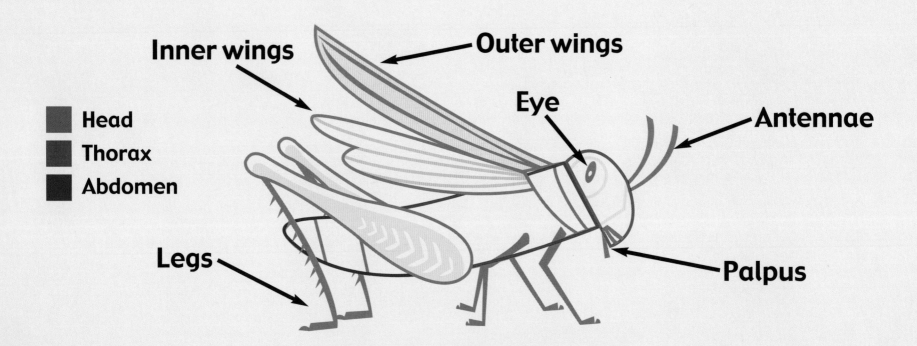

Inner wings
Outer wings
Eye
Antennae
Head
Thorax
Abdomen
Legs
Palpus

Fun Facts

- There are about 9,000 kinds of grasshoppers.

- Most grasshoppers are brown or green, but some grasshoppers in tropical areas have much brighter colors.

- A grasshopper's antennae sometimes are called horns. There are two main families of grasshoppers: short-horned and long-horned. The grasshoppers in this book are short-horned. Long-horned grasshoppers, such as katydids, have antennae that are longer than their bodies!

- Grasshoppers spit out a brown liquid when they are attacked or picked up. This is called tobacco juice.

- A grasshopper's jaws move from side to side, not up and down the way yours do.

Make a Grasshopper Pie

Have you ever heard of grasshopper pie? It's not made of grasshoppers, but it did get its name from the green and brown grasshopper colors. The pie is green and fluffy and is flavored with mint. It has a chocolate crust.

Here's an easy version of grasshopper pie you can make at home. All you need is whipped topping, green food coloring, peppermint extract, chocolate graham crackers, and chocolate chips.

Thaw some frozen whipped topping. Stir in a few drops of green food coloring and a drop of peppermint extract. Spread the topping over some chocolate graham crackers. Decorate with chocolate chips. Put your pie in the freezer until it's firm. Then enjoy!

(If you don't have whipped topping, you could try melted marshmallows. Then you wouldn't need to freeze it.)

Words to Know

antennae–Antennae (an-TEN-ee) are feelers on an insect's head. Antennae is the word for more than one antenna (an-TEN-uh).

larvae–Newly hatched flies are called larvae (LAR-vee). They look like worms. Larvae is the word for more than one larva.

mate–Male and female grasshoppers mate by joining together special parts of their bodies. After they've mated, the female can lay eggs.

molt–When a grasshopper molts, its outer shell comes off. A new shell is beneath it. Molting is part of growing up for grasshoppers.

nymph–A nymph is a small, young grasshopper.

palpi–Palpi (PALP-ee) are small feelers on a grasshopper's mouth that hold and taste food. Palpi is the word for more than one palpus.

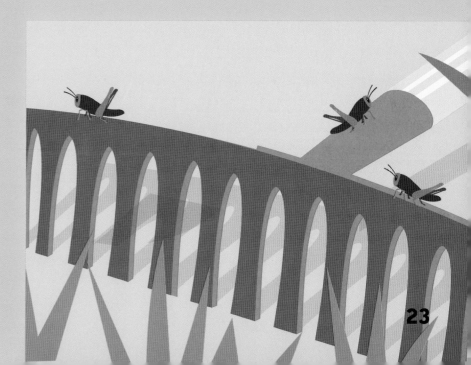

To Learn More

At the Library

Allen, Judy. *Are You a Grasshopper?* New York: Kingfisher, 2002.

Heinrichs, Ann. *Grasshoppers.* Minneapolis: Compass Point Books, 2002.

Lobel, Arnold. *Grasshopper on the Road.* New York: Harper & Row, 1978.

Williams, Sheron. *Imani's Music.* New York: Atheneum, 2000.

On the Web

enature.com
http://www.enature.com/guides/select_Insects_and_Spiders.asp
Articles about and photos of almost 300 species of insects and spiders

The National Park Service
http://www1.nature.nps.gov/wv/insects.htm
A guide to finding and studying insects at national parks

University of Kentucky Department of Entomology
http://www.uky.edu/Agriculture/Entomology/ythfacts/entyouth.htm
A kid-friendly site with insect games, jokes, articles, and resources

Fact Hound
Fact Hound offers a safe, fun way to find Web sites related to this book. All of the sites on Fact Hound have been researched by our staff.
http://www.facthound.com

1. Visit the Fact Hound home page.

2. Enter a search word related to this book, or type in this special code: 140480143X.

3. Click on the FETCH IT button.

Your trusty Fact Hound will fetch the best sites for you!

Index